# The

# REVERSE

# SPELLING

## CHALLENGE

### By Lee Zander

**TWORAVENS**
BOOKS

# Special Thanks To
## Remesch & Alexis

**Xander & Rem**
Children's Coloring & Activity Books

Paperback Edition: 9781960320483
Digital Edition: 9781960320506

Published in the United States by Two Ravens Books LLC,

254 Chapman Rd, Ste 209, Newark DE 19702

'Expand the mind, free the imagination, one title at a time.'
**www.tworavensbooks.com**

Get ready for a hilarious, fast-paced spelling challenge - in reverse!

# The Reverse Spelling Challenge

## A Hilarious, Silly, and Challenging Word Game Book (For 2-4 Players)

**AGES 10+**

## Setup:

- Decide if playing individually or in teams.

- Set a round limit (e.g. five rounds) or a point goal (e.g. first to 10 points).

- Agree on a difficulty level (e.g. start on the **Easy** level).

# How to Play:

1. One player (or team) becomes the **'Word Giver'**.

2. The **Word Giver** starts from the top of a chosen page and says a word. The next player (or team member from the opposite team) attempts to spell it backward aloud without writing it down.

3. Correct reverse-spelling earns a point. An incorrect attempt or refusal to spell means the player lose their turn, and don't earn any points.

4. If a mistake is made or the player refuses to spell, they must perform the **"Silly Act"**.

5. After each round, the role of the Word Giver rotates to the next player or team.

## WINNING:
- **For individual play:** The player with the most points after all rounds is declared the winner.

- **For team play:** The team with the most combined points at the end wins.

**REMEMBER:** The primary aim is fun and improving reverse-spelling skills! Adjust the rules as desired to suit the group, and enjoy the challenge!

# TABLE OF CONTENTS

# EASY
# LEVEL

# Easy
## LEVEL

**Points**

## SPARK ⬌ K-R-A-P-S     1

**SILLY ACT:** Pretend to start a campfire!

## TRUST ⬌ T-S-U-R-T     1

**SILLY ACT:** Pretend to catch a falling friend!

## JUMPS ⬌ S-P-M-U-J     1

**SILLY ACT:** Mimic jumping over an invisible rope!

## GRASP ⬌ P-S-A-R-G     1

**SILLY ACT:** Pretend to reach and grasp an imaginary object above you!

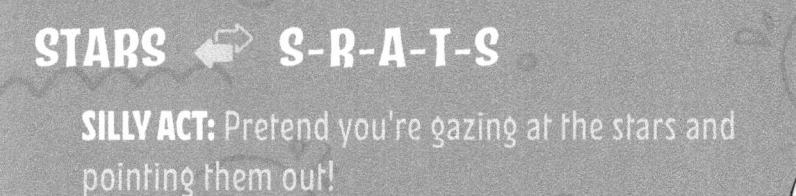

## STARS ⬌ S-R-A-T-S     6

**SILLY ACT:** Pretend you're gazing at the stars and pointing them out!

#  Easy
### LEVEL

**Points**

## FLAME ⇦ E-M-A-L-F      1

**SILLY ACT:** Pretend to warm your hands over a fire!

## SKATE ⇦ E-T-A-K-S      1

**SILLY ACT:** Pretend to ice skate around the room!

## BRAIN ⇦ N-I-A-R-B      1

**SILLY ACT:** Scratch your head in deep thought!

## PRINT ⇦ T-N-I-R-P      1

**SILLY ACT:** Pretend to stuff a huge stack of paper into a tiny printer!

## PLANT ⇦ T-N-A-L-P      6

**SILLY ACT:** Pretend to dig a hole and plant a seed!

# Easy

## LEVEL

**Points**

## COAST ⇨ T-S-A-O-C          1

**SILLY ACT:** Pretend you're at the beach, skipping stones on the water!

## CRASH ⇦ H-S-A-R-C          1

**SILLY ACT:** Pretend you're a cymbal in an orchestra and crash loudly!

## TRACK ⇦ K-C-A-R-T          1

**SILLY ACT:** Pretend to run on a racetrack, complete with start and finish!

## SHELF ⇨ F-L-E-H-S          1

**SILLY ACT:** Pretend to place books on an imaginary shelf!

## TWIST ⇄ T-S-I-W-T          6

**SILLY ACT:** Do the twist dance!

#  Easy
## LEVEL

**Points**

## SWIFT ⇄ T-F-I-W-S

1

**SILLY ACT:** Run on the spot as fast as you can!

## CREAK ⇄ K-A-E-R-C

1

**SILLY ACT:** Walk like you're on old creaky floorboards!

## GHOST ⇄ T-S-O-H-G

1

**SILLY ACT:** Pretend you're a ghost floating around the room!

## SMOKE ⇄ E-K-O-M-S

1

**SILLY ACT:** Pretend to wave away smoke from an imaginary fire!

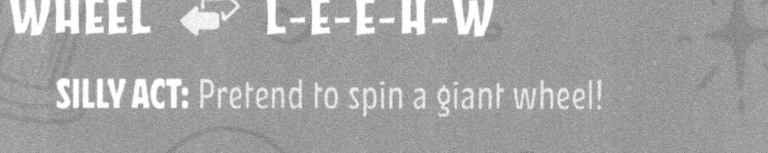

## WHEEL ⇄ L-E-E-H-W

6

**SILLY ACT:** Pretend to spin a giant wheel!

#  Easy
## LEVEL

**Points**

## STACK ⬅ K-C-A-T-S      1

**SILLY ACT:** Pretend to stack invisible blocks as high as you can!

## FLUTE ⬅ E-T-U-L-F      1

**SILLY ACT:** Pretend to play an imaginary flute!

## CHALK ⬅ K-L-A-H-C      1

**SILLY ACT:** Pretend to write on a huge chalkboard!

## SQUAT ⬅ T-A-U-Q-S      1

**SILLY ACT:** Do 10 squats!

## STICK ⬅ K-C-I-T-S      6

**SILLY ACT:** Pretend to walk with a big walking stick!

#  Easy
## LEVEL

**Points**

## CLOTH ⇦ H-T-O-L-C          1

**SILLY ACT:** Pretend to fold an enormous piece of cloth!

## FRONT ⇦ T-N-O-R-F          1

**SILLY ACT:** Pretend to push something heavy to the front!

## SWING ⇦ G-N-I-W-S          1

**SILLY ACT:** Pretend you're swinging high on a playground swing!

## BRICK ⇦ K-C-I-R-B          1

**SILLY ACT:** Pretend to build a wall with heavy bricks!

## GRANT ⇦ T-N-A-R-G          6

**SILLY ACT:** Pretend you're granting wishes like a fairy!

# Easy
## LEVEL

**Points**

## FROST ⇦ T-S-O-R-F        1

**SILLY ACT:** Pretend to shiver like you're in a frosty winter!

## STAMP ⇦ P-M-A-T-S        1

**SILLY ACT:** Pretend to lick a stamp and place it on an envelope!

## SWEPT ⇦ T-P-E-W-S        1

**SILLY ACT:** Pretend to sweep the floor with a big broom!

## SNACK ⇦ K-C-A-N-S        1

**SILLY ACT:** Pretend to eat your favorite snack!

## FLICK ⇦ K-C-I-L-F        6

**SILLY ACT:** Pretend to flick invisible bugs away!

 # Easy
### LEVEL

**Points**

## CRUST ⇦ T-S-U-R-C

1

**SILLY ACT:** Pretend to cut and eat a slice of pie!

## DRAFT ⇦ T-F-A-R-D

1

**SILLY ACT:** Pretend you're being blown away by a strong draft of wind!

## GLINT ⇦ T-N-I-L-G

1

**SILLY ACT:** Pretend to be dazzled by a shiny object!

## FISH ⇦ H-S-I-F

1

**SILLY ACT:** Swim in place like a fish!

## FRISK ⇦ K-S-I-R-F

6

**SILLY ACT:** Pretend to be a police officer frisking an invisible suspect!

# Easy

**LEVEL**

**Points**

## BLUNT ⟷ T-N-U-L-B     1

**SILLY ACT:** Pretend to be trying to cut something with a very blunt knife!

## SCRAP ⟷ P-A-R-C-S     1

**SILLY ACT:** Pretend to tear a piece of paper into tiny scraps!

## FLASK ⟷ K-S-A-L-F     1

**SILLY ACT:** Pretend you're a scientist mixing chemicals in a flask!

## CLEFT ⟷ T-F-E-L-C     1

**SILLY ACT:** Pretend to be climbing a steep mountain with a deep cleft!

## TREE ⟷ E-E-R-T     6

**SILLY ACT:** Stand tall and sway like a tree in the wind!

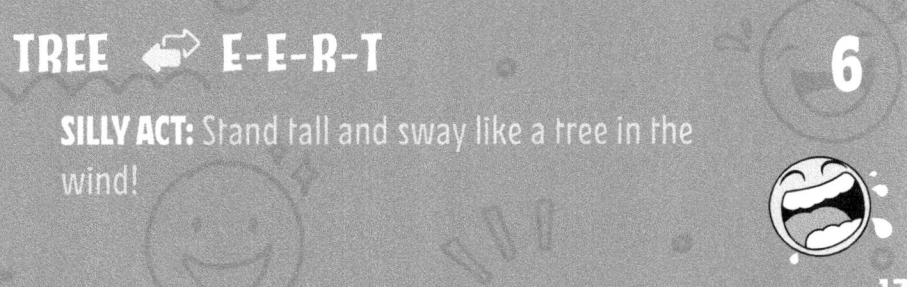

#  Easy
### LEVEL

**Points**

## GRUNT ⇦ T-N-U-R-G          1

**SILLY ACT:** Pretend to be a pig and give your best grunt!

## SKULK ⇦ K-L-U-K-S          1

**SILLY ACT:** Pretend to be a sneaky creature skulking in the shadows!

## GULPS ⇦ S-P-L-U-G          1

**SILLY ACT:** Pretend you're very thirsty and take huge gulps of an imaginary drink!

## BRISK ⇦ K-S-I-R-B          1

**SILLY ACT:** Pretend to walk briskly against a strong wind!

## SHARP ⇦ P-R-A-H-S          6

**SILLY ACT:** Pretend to prick your finger on something very sharp!

# Easy

**LEVEL**

**Points**

## STRAP ⟺ P-A-R-T-S     1

**SILLY ACT:** Pretend to tighten a big strap around an invisible box!

## DRAPE ⟺ E-P-A-R-D     1

**SILLY ACT:** Pretend to hang a giant drape!

## STAGE ⟺ E-G-A-T-S     1

**SILLY ACT:** Perform an air guitar solo on an imaginary stage!

## CRAFT ⟺ T-F-A-R-C     1

**SILLY ACT:** Pretend to be gluing and cutting for a craft project!

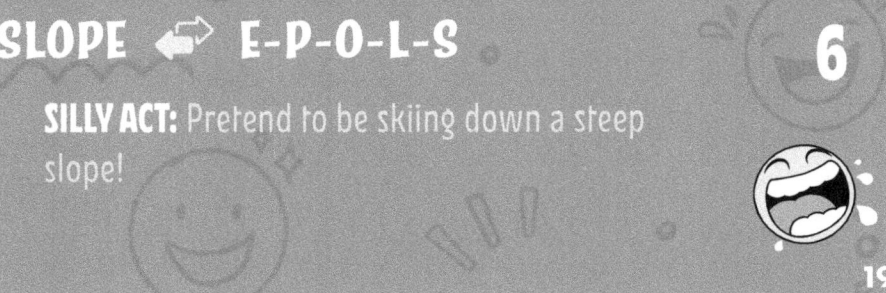

## SLOPE ⟺ E-P-O-L-S     6

**SILLY ACT:** Pretend to be skiing down a steep slope!

# Easy
### LEVEL

**Points**

## TRUCK ⬅ K-C-U-R-T
**1**

**SILLY ACT:** Pretend to drive a large truck!

## GLAZE ⬅ E-Z-A-L-G
**1**

**SILLY ACT:** Pretend to paint glaze on a giant pottery bowl!

## PLUMB ⬅ B-M-U-L-P
**1**

**SILLY ACT:** Pretend to be a plumber fixing a pipe!

## CRUMB ⬅ B-M-U-R-C
**1**

**SILLY ACT:** Pretend to be a bird picking up crumbs!

## FLINT ⬅ T-N-I-L-F
**6**

**SILLY ACT:** Pretend to start a fire with a piece of flint!

# Easy
## LEVEL

| | Points |
|---|---|
| **BALL** ⇄ **L-L-A-B** | 1 |

**SILLY ACT:** Pretend to dribble a basketball then make a slam dunk!

| | |
|---|---|
| **GRACE** ⇄ **E-C-A-R-G** | 1 |

**SILLY ACT:** Dance gracefully across the room!

| | |
|---|---|
| **BRAGS** ⇄ **S-G-A-R-B** | 1 |

**SILLY ACT:** Boast about an imaginary victory!

| | |
|---|---|
| **FLASH** ⇄ **H-S-A-L-F** | 1 |

**SILLY ACT:** Pretend to be startled by a sudden flash of light!

| | |
|---|---|
| **SCRUB** ⇄ **B-U-R-C-S** | 6 |

**SILLY ACT:** Pretend to scrub a huge dirty pot!

#  Easy
## LEVEL

**Points**

### SWARM ⇄ M-R-A-W-S
**1**

**SILLY ACT:** Pretend to shoo away a swarm of bees!

### SCORN ⇄ N-R-O-C-S
**1**

**SILLY ACT:** Pretend to scorn an imaginary bad joke!

### DROWN ⇄ N-W-O-R-D
**1**

**SILLY ACT:** Pretend to swim in deep water!

### CROWD ⇄ D-W-O-R-C
**1**

**SILLY ACT:** Pretend to wave at a big crowd!

### CAKE ⇄ E-K-A-C
**6**

**SILLY ACT:** Pretend to slice a large piece of cake and take a big bite!

# Easy

**LEVEL**

**Points**

## SWEEP ⇦ P-E-E-W-S     1

**SILLY ACT:** Pretend to sweep the floor!

## CLOAK ⇦ K-A-O-L-C     1

**SILLY ACT:** Pretend to disappear with a magic cloak!

## STRAY ⇦ Y-A-R-T-S     1

**SILLY ACT:** Pretend to be a lost puppy!

## CRANK ⇦ K-N-A-R-C     1

**SILLY ACT:** Pretend to turn a large crank!

## FLOUR ⇦ R-U-O-L-F     6

**SILLY ACT:** Pretend to knead a large batch of dough!

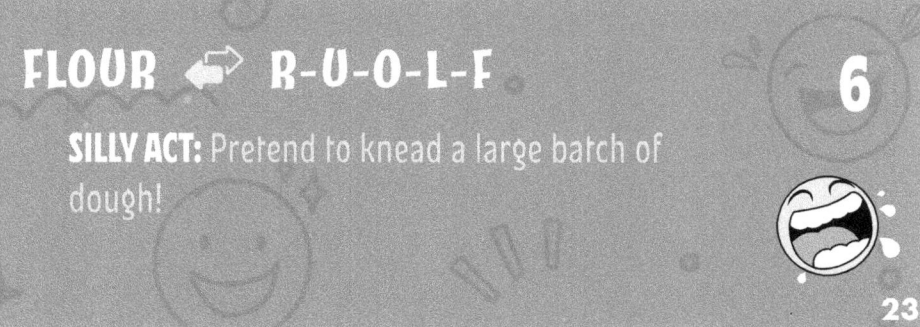

#  Easy
### LEVEL

**Points**

## STEAL ⟺ L-A-E-T-S     1
**SILLY ACT:** Pretend to sneak and steal a jewel!

## GRIND ⟺ D-N-I-R-G     1
**SILLY ACT:** Pretend to grind coffee beans!

## SWANK ⟺ K-N-A-W-S     1
**SILLY ACT:** Walk around with swank and swagger!

## STERN ⟺ N-R-E-T-S     1
**SILLY ACT:** Pretend to steer a ship from the stern!

## CROWN ⟺ N-W-O-R-C     6
**SILLY ACT:** Pretend to place a crown on your head!

# Easy
## LEVEL

**Points**

## GLARE ⇦ E-R-A-L-G          1

**SILLY ACT:** Pretend to shield your eyes from a bright glare!

## STOVE ⇦ E-V-O-T-S          1

**SILLY ACT:** Pretend to cook a feast on a miniature stove!

## SWAMP ⇦ P-M-A-W-S          1

**SILLY ACT:** Pretend to slog through a muddy swamp!

## SWIRL ⇦ L-R-I-W-S          1

**SILLY ACT:** Pretend to stir a giant pot of soup!

## FRESH ⇦ H-S-E-R-F          6

**SILLY ACT:** Pretend to pick fresh fruit from a tree!

# Easy

## LEVEL

**Points**

**CRISP** ⬌ **P-S-I-R-C**    **1**

**SILLY ACT:** Pretend to bite into a crispy apple!

**STUFF** ⬌ **F-F-U-T-S**    **1**

**SILLY ACT:** Pretend to stuff a giant turkey!

**DWELL** ⬌ **L-L-E-W-D**    **1**

**SILLY ACT:** Pretend to unlock the door to your dream home!

**CRAMP** ⬌ **P-M-A-R-C**    **1**

**SILLY ACT:** Pretend to get a sudden leg cramp!

**DWARF** ⬌ **F-R-A-W-D**    **6**

**SILLY ACT:** Pretend to be a dwarf digging for gems!

# Easy

### LEVEL

**Points**

**FLAKE** ⮂ **E-K-A-L-F**    1

**SILLY ACT:** Pretend to catch snowflakes on your tongue!

**GROVE** ⮂ **E-V-O-R-G**    1

**SILLY ACT:** Pretend to walk through an orange grove!

**CRAWL** ⮂ **L-W-A-R-C**    1

**SILLY ACT:** Crawl like an ant around the room.

**STORK** ⮂ **K-R-O-T-S**    1

**SILLY ACT:** Walk like a stork, lifting your knees high.

**FROGS** ⮂ **S-G-O-R-F**    6

**SILLY ACT:** Leap like a frog.

# Easy
## LEVEL

**Points**

### CLOUD ➡ D-U-O-L-C     1

**SILLY ACT:** Move gracefully across the room like a floating cloud.

### STAIR ➡ R-I-A-T-S     1

**SILLY ACT:** Pretend to climb an imaginary staircase.

### DRAIN ➡ N-I-A-R-D     1

**SILLY ACT:** Pretend to unclog an imaginary drain.

### QUACK ➡ K-C-A-U-Q     1

**SILLY ACT:** Waddle and quack like a duck.

### SPOOK ➡ K-O-O-P-S     6

**SILLY ACT:** Act like a ghost and try to spook someone.

# Easy
### LEVEL

**Points**

## WHISK ⇦ K-S-I-H-W
**1**

**SILLY ACT:** Pretend to whisk an imaginary bowl of batter.

## DROPS ⇦ S-P-O-R-D
**1**

**SILLY ACT:** Pretend to dodge raindrops falling from the sky.

## WHARF ⇦ F-R-A-H-W
**1**

**SILLY ACT:** Pretend to reel in a big fish from an imaginary wharf.

## BLINK ⇦ K-N-I-L-B
**1**

**SILLY ACT:** Blink your eyes rapidly as if something is in your eye.

## PRIZE ⇦ E-Z-I-R-P
**6**

**SILLY ACT:** Pretend to open an imaginary gift with excitement.

# MEDIUM
# LEVEL

# Medium

## LEVEL

**Points**

**CAPTURE** ⇦ E-R-U-T-P-A-C    1

**SILLY ACT:** Pretend to catch a butterfly!

**JOURNEY** ⇦ Y-E-N-R-U-O-J    1

**SILLY ACT:** Act like you're climbing a huge mountain!

**FICTION** ⇦ N-O-I-T-C-I-F    1

**SILLY ACT:** Pretend to read a thrilling book aloud!

**ELEPHANT** ⇦ T-N-A-H-P-E-L-E    1

**SILLY ACT:** Stomp and trumpet like an elephant!

**GLORIOUS** ⇦ S-U-O-I-R-O-L-G    **6**

**SILLY ACT:** Pretend you've just won a trophy!

# Medium
## LEVEL

**Points**

### AMAZING ⇦ G-N-I-Z-A-M-A     1

**SILLY ACT:** Express surprise and amazement!

### ORGANIZE ⇦ E-Z-I-N-A-G-R-O     1

**SILLY ACT:** Pretend to tidy up a messy room!

### EDUCATION ⇦ N-O-I-T-A-C-U-D-E     1

**SILLY ACT:** Act like a strict teacher!

### CONFIDENT ⇦ T-N-E-D-I-F-N-O-C     1

**SILLY ACT:** Walk and talk with exaggerated confidence!

### ADVENTURE ⇦ E-R-U-T-N-E-V-D-A     6

**SILLY ACT:** Pretend you're exploring a jungle!

# Medium
### LEVEL

**Points**

## RESILIENT ⬄ T-N-E-I-L-I-S-E-R    1

**SILLY ACT:** Pretend to bounce back after a fall!

## UNIVERSE ⬄ E-S-R-E-V-I-N-U    1

**SILLY ACT:** Pretend to float in space!

## EXCELLENT ⬄ T-N-E-L-L-E-C-X-E    1

**SILLY ACT:** Give two thumbs up while making a silly face!

## DAUGHTER ⬄ R-E-T-H-G-U-A-D    1

**SILLY ACT:** Pretend to cradle a baby!

## ORIGINAL ⬄ L-A-N-I-G-I-R-O    6

**SILLY ACT:** Invent a dance move on the spot!

# Medium

## LEVEL

**Points**

**DISASTER** ➡️ R-E-T-S-A-S-I-D    1

**SILLY ACT:** Pretend to balance during an earthquake!

**SQUIRREL** ⬅️ L-E-R-R-I-U-Q-S    1

**SILLY ACT:** Mimic gathering acorns like a squirrel!

**LANTERN** ➡️ N-R-E-T-N-A-L    1

**SILLY ACT:** Pretend to light a lantern in the dark!

**SYMMETRY** ⬅️ Y-R-T-E-M-M-Y-S    1

**SILLY ACT:** Mimic mirroring your own movements!

**CURRENCY** ➡️ Y-C-N-E-R-R-U-C    6

**SILLY ACT:** Pretend to count a large stack of bills!

# Medium
## LEVEL

**Points**

**TANGERINE** ⬅️ E-N-I-R-E-G-N-A-T    1

**SILLY ACT:** Pretend to peel and eat a juicy tangerine!

**LIGHTNING** ⬅️ G-N-I-N-T-H-G-I-L    1

**SILLY ACT:** Pretend to be shocked by a sudden lightning bolt!

**UMBRELLA** ⬅️ A-L-L-E-R-B-M-U    1

**SILLY ACT:** Pretend to open and spin an umbrella!

**RADIATOR** ⬅️ R-O-T-A-I-D-A-R    1

**SILLY ACT:** Act like you're warming your hands by a radiator!

**KEYBOARD** ⬅️ D-R-A-O-B-Y-E-K    **6**

**SILLY ACT:** Pretend to play a piano!

# Medium

## LEVEL

**Points**

### EXPLORER ⇨ R-E-R-O-L-P-X-E 1

**SILLY ACT:** Act as if you're looking far off into the distance with binoculars!

### DETECTIVE ⇦ E-V-I-T-C-E-T-E-D 1

**SILLY ACT:** Pretend to use a magnifying glass to inspect something!

### SUNSHINE ⇨ E-N-I-H-S-N-U-S 1

**SILLY ACT:** Pretend you're shielding your eyes from bright light!

### SURPRISE ⇨ E-S-I-R-P-R-U-S 1

**SILLY ACT:** Act shocked as you've just been surprised!

### REMEMBER ⇦ R-E-B-M-E-M-E-R 6

**SILLY ACT:** Act like you're trying hard to remember something!

# Medium
## LEVEL

**Points**

**BACKPACK** ⬅ **K-C-A-P-K-C-A-B**  1

**SILLY ACT:** Pretend you're struggling to lift a heavy backpack!

**FLAMINGO** ⬅ **O-G-N-I-M-A-L-F**  1

**SILLY ACT:** Stand on one leg like a flamingo!

**GALAXIES** ⬅ **S-E-I-X-A-L-A-G**  1

**SILLY ACT:** Spin slowly in a circle, pretending to be a galaxy!

**HAMBURGER** ⬅ **R-E-G-R-U-B-M-A-H**  1

**SILLY ACT:** Mime cooking and flipping a hamburger!

**DISPATCH** ⬅ **H-C-T-A-P-S-I-D**  6

**SILLY ACT:** Pretend to be a dispatcher, sending out imaginary emergency vehicles!

# Medium

### LEVEL

**Points**

## IMAGINARY ⬅ Y-R-A-N-I-G-A-M-I    1

**SILLY ACT:** Interact with an imaginary friend!

## JUBILANT ⬅ T-N-A-L-I-B-U-J    1

**SILLY ACT:** Jump up and down in joy!

## KINGDOMS ⬅ S-M-O-D-G-N-I-K    1

**SILLY ACT:** Mimic a king or queen addressing their kingdom!

## LANTERNS ⬅ S-N-R-E-T-N-A-L    1

**SILLY ACT:** Pretend you're holding a lantern in the dark!

## MAJORITY ⬅ Y-T-I-R-O-J-A-M    6

**SILLY ACT:** Pretend to be a judge making a decision based on a majority vote.

# Medium

### LEVEL

**Points**

## NIGHTINGALE ⬅️ E-L-A-G-N-I-T-H-G-I-N    1

**SILLY ACT:** Imitate a bird singing!

## OBSTACLE ⬅️ E-L-C-A-T-S-B-O    1

**SILLY ACT:** Pretend to overcome an imaginary obstacle course!

## PARACHUTE ⬅️ E-T-U-H-C-A-R-A-P    1

**SILLY ACT:** Pretend to pull a parachute cord and float down!

## QUESTIONS ⬅️ S-N-O-I-T-S-E-U-Q    1

**SILLY ACT:** Act like you're on a quiz show, pondering a tricky question!

## RADIATION ⬅️ N-O-I-T-A-I-D-A-R    6

**SILLY ACT:** Pretend you're a scientist working with a Geiger counter!

#  Medium
## LEVEL

**Points**

**SATELLITE** ⬅ E-T-I-L-L-E-T-A-S     1

**SILLY ACT:** Pretend you are a satellite circling the Earth.

**TRANSFORM** ⬅ M-R-O-F-S-N-A-R-T     1

**SILLY ACT:** Act out, transforming into a robot!

**UNDERWEAR** ⬅ R-A-E-W-R-E-D-N-U     1

**SILLY ACT:** Pretend you're getting dressed!

**VACATIONS** ⬅ S-N-O-I-T-A-C-A-V     1

**SILLY ACT:** Act like you're lounging on a beach!

**WILDERNESS** ⬅ S-S-E-N-R-E-D-L-I-W     6

**SILLY ACT:** Act like you're exploring the wilderness with binoculars!

# Medium

## LEVEL

**Points**

**XENOPHOBIA** ⇦ A-I-B-O-H-P-O-N-E-X          1

**SILLY ACT:** Act like you're a world traveler meeting new cultures!

**ZUCCHINI** ⇦ I-N-I-H-C-C-U-Z          1

**SILLY ACT:** Pretend you're cooking with a lot of zucchini!

**ALGORITHM** ⇦ M-H-T-I-R-O-G-L-A          1

**SILLY ACT:** Pretend you're a computer processing information!

**BILLOWING** ⇦ G-N-I-W-O-L-L-I-B          1

**SILLY ACT:** Pretend you're a cloud growing larger and larger!

**YESTERYEAR** ⇦ R-A-E-Y-R-E-T-S-E-Y          6

**SILLY ACT:** Pretend you're an old person reminiscing about the "good old days"!

# Medium

### LEVEL

**Points**

## CAMPAIGNER ⇨ R-E-N-G-I-A-P-M-A-C  1

**SILLY ACT:** Act like you're giving an impassioned political speech!

## DANGEROUS ⇦ S-U-O-R-E-G-N-A-D  1

**SILLY ACT:** Pretend you're a stunt performer doing a dangerous trick!

## FRAGMENTED ⇨ D-E-T-N-E-M-G-A-R-F  1

**SILLY ACT:** Act like you're putting together a puzzle!

## GRAVITATIONAL ⇨ L-A-N-O-I-T-A-T-I-V-A-R-G  1

**SILLY ACT:** Pretend a super-strong gravitational force is pulling you down!

## ELONGATED ⇨ D-E-T-A-G-N-O-L-E  6

**SILLY ACT:** Stretch like you're a piece of silly putty being pulled longer and longer!

# Medium
## LEVEL

**Points**

## HESITATION ⇦ N-O-I-T-A-T-I-S-E-H ⟶ 1

**SILLY ACT:** Act like you need more time to decide about making a choice!

## ILLUMINATE ⇦ E-T-A-N-I-M-U-L-L-I ⟶ 1

**SILLY ACT:** Pretend you're holding a flashlight and illuminating a dark space!

## JUXTAPOSED ⇦ D-E-S-O-P-A-T-X-U-J ⟶ 1

**SILLY ACT:** Position two imaginary objects side by side to compare them!

## LIQUIDATION ⇦ N-O-I-T-A-D-I-U-Q-I-L ⟶ 1

**SILLY ACT:** Pretend you're a liquid flowing downhill!

## KALEIDOSCOPE ⇦ E-P-O-C-S-O-D-I-E-L-A-K ⟶ 6

**SILLY ACT:** Pretend you're looking through a kaleidoscope and being amazed by the changing patterns!

# Medium

## LEVEL

**Points**

**NAVIGATIONAL** ⬌ L-A-N-O-I-T-A-G-I-V-A-N   **1**

**SILLY ACT:** Pretend you're a sailor navigating through a stormy sea!

**OBSERVATIONS** ⬌ S-N-O-I-T-A-V-R-E-S-B-O   **1**

**SILLY ACT:** Act like a detective, observing a mysterious scene for clues!

**PERSPECTIVES** ⬌ S-E-V-I-T-C-E-P-S-R-E-P   **1**

**SILLY ACT:** Pretend you're looking at an object from different angles!

**QUARANTINED** ⬌ D-E-N-I-T-N-A-R-A-U-Q   **1**

**SILLY ACT:** Pretend you're stuck in a bubble, unable to touch anything around you!

**MISUNDERSTAND** ⬌ D-N-A-T-S-R-E-D-N-U-S-I-M   **6**

**SILLY ACT:** Act like you're confused about the instructions you've been given!

# Medium

## LEVEL

**Points**

**REFRIGERATE** ⇦ E-T-A-R-E-G-I-R-F-E-R  **1**

**SILLY ACT:** Pretend you're getting super cold like you're in a refrigerator!

**SPECULATIVE** ⇦ E-V-I-T-A-L-U-C-E-P-S  **1**

**SILLY ACT:** Pretend you're deep in thought, pondering a difficult question!

**TELEVISION** ⇦ N-O-I-S-I-V-E-L-E-T  **1**

**SILLY ACT:** Pretend you're flipping through channels on a TV!

**VACCINATION** ⇨ N-O-I-T-A-N-I-C-C-A-V  **1**

**SILLY ACT:** Pretend you're a doctor giving a shot!

**UNWARRANTED** ⇦ D-E-T-N-A-R-R-A-W-N-U  **6**

**SILLY ACT:** Act as if you've received a surprise!

# Medium
## LEVEL

**Points**

**WEATHERIZED** ⇦ D-E-Z-I-R-E-H-T-A-E-W    1

**SILLY ACT:** Pretend you're getting bundled up for a winter storm!

**XEROGRAPHY** ⇦ Y-H-P-A-R-G-O-R-E-X    1

**SILLY ACT:** Pretend you're a copier, duplicating a document!

**YACHTSMEN** ⇦ N-E-M-S-T-H-C-A-Y    1

**SILLY ACT:** Pretend you're sailing a yacht on a breezy day!

**ZIGZAGGING** ⇦ G-N-I-G-G-A-Z-G-I-Z    1

**SILLY ACT:** Zigzag around as if you're avoiding obstacles!

**HANDKERCHIEF** ⇦ F-E-I-H-C-R-E-K-D-N-A-H    6

**SILLY ACT:** Pretend to sneeze and wipe your nose with an invisible handkerchief.

# Medium
## LEVEL

**Points**

### DOLPHIN ⟵ N-I-H-P-L-O-D          1

**SILLY ACT:** Leap like a dolphin out of the water.

### PINEAPPLE ⟵ E-L-P-P-A-E-N-I-P          1

**SILLY ACT:** Mime cutting open a pineapple and tasting it.

### BLUEBERRY ⟵ Y-R-R-E-B-E-U-L-B          1

**SILLY ACT:** Pretend to pick and eat imaginary blueberries.

### MICROSCOPE ⟵ E-P-O-C-S-O-R-C-I-M          1

**SILLY ACT:** Pretend to look through a microscope and discover something amazing!

### LIGHTHOUSE ⟵ E-S-U-O-H-T-H-G-I-L          6

**SILLY ACT:** Act like a lighthouse, spinning in place with your arms extended like a beacon.

# Medium

## LEVEL

**Points**

**BUTTERFLY** ⬅ Y-L-F-R-E-T-T-U-B    1

**SILLY ACT:** Flap your arms like a butterfly.

**STRAWBERRY** ⬅ Y-R-R-E-B-W-A-R-T-S   1

**SILLY ACT:** Pretend to pick and eat imaginary strawberries.

**LADDER** ⬅ R-E-D-D-A-L    1

**SILLY ACT:** Pretend to climb a really tall ladder.

**BROCCOLI** ⬅ I-L-O-C-C-O-R-B    1

**SILLY ACT:** Pretend to eat a giant piece of broccoli, stem and all.

**SKATEBOARD** ⬅ D-R-A-O-B-E-T-A-K-S   6

**SILLY ACT:** Pretend to ride a skateboard and do a trick.

# Medium

### LEVEL

**Points**

## PENGUIN ➡ N-I-U-G-N-E-P    1

**SILLY ACT:** Waddle and flap your arms like a penguin.

## DUMBBELL ➡ L-L-E-B-B-M-U-D    1

**SILLY ACT:** Pretend to lift a really heavy dumbbell.

## JELLYFISH ➡ H-S-I-F-Y-L-L-E-J    1

**SILLY ACT:** Float and wobble like a jellyfish.

## DINOSAUR ➡ R-U-A-S-O-N-I-D    1

**SILLY ACT:** Act like a dinosaur, roaring and stomping around.

## CROCODILE ➡ E-L-I-D-O-C-O-R-C    6

**SILLY ACT:** Open and close your arms wide like a crocodile's mouth.

# Medium

## LEVEL

**Points**

### UNICYCLE ⬅ E-L-C-Y-C-I-N-U        1

**SILLY ACT:** Pretend to ride a unicycle, trying to keep your balance.

### KANGAROO ⬅ O-O-R-A-G-N-A-K        1

**SILLY ACT:** Hop around like a kangaroo.

### OCTOPUS ⬅ S-U-P-O-T-C-O        1

**SILLY ACT:** Pretend to be an octopus, waving your eight arms around.

### TRAMPOLINE ⬅ E-N-I-L-O-P-M-A-R-T        1

**SILLY ACT:** Pretend to jump on a trampoline, getting higher with each jump!

### DISHWASHER ⬅ R-E-H-S-A-W-H-S-I-D        6

**SILLY ACT:** Mime loading a dishwasher, bending and placing dishes carefully.

# Medium
## LEVEL

**Points**

### SNOWBOARD ⇦ D-R-A-O-B-W-O-N-S    1

**SILLY ACT:** Pretend to ride a snowboard, carving down a snowy mountain.

### SPAGHETTI ⇦ I-T-T-E-H-G-A-P-S    1

**SILLY ACT:** Pretend to twirl and eat a big plate of spaghetti.

### PARTICIPATE ⇦ E-T-A-P-I-C-I-T-R-A-P    1

**SILLY ACT:** Act like you're enthusiastically participating in a game!

### INVESTIGATE ⇦ E-T-A-G-I-T-S-E-V-N-I    1

**SILLY ACT:** Pretend to start a campfire!

### CAPTIVATE ⇦ E-T-A-V-I-T-P-A-C    6

**SILLY ACT:** Pretend to be a magician mesmerizing an audience with a magic trick!

# HARD

# LEVEL

# Hard

### LEVEL

## Points

**APPRECIATION** ← N-O-I-T-A-I-C-E-R-P-P-A   1

**SILLY ACT:** Pretend to open a gift and show how grateful you are!

**CONTROVERSIAL** ← L-A-I-S-R-E-V-O-R-T-N-O-C   1

**SILLY ACT:** Act out a debate, presenting both sides of an argument.

**BATTLEGROUND** ← D-N-U-O-R-G-E-L-T-T-A-B   1

**SILLY ACT:** Mime a battle scene with your imaginary sword and shield.

**ACKNOWLEDGEMENT** ← T-N-E-M-E-G-D-E-L-W-O-N-K-C-A   1

**SILLY ACT:** Pretend to write a thank you note and hand it to someone.

**ENCOURAGEMENT** ← T-N-E-M-E-G-A-R-U-O-C-N-E   6

**SILLY ACT:** Be a cheerleader, and come up with a quick cheer!

# Hard
## LEVEL

## Points

**IMPRESSIONABLE** ← E-L-B-A-N-O-I-S-S-E-R-P-M-I    1

**SILLY ACT:** Pretend to be a statue mimicking different poses.

**CIRCUMNAVIGATE** ← E-T-A-G-I-V-A-N-M-U-C-R-I-C    1

**SILLY ACT:** Pretend to be a sailor, steering your ship around the globe.

**APPRECIATIVE** ← E-V-I-T-A-I-C-E-R-P-P-A    1

**SILLY ACT:** Clap your hands and cheer to show appreciation.

**PRECIPITATION** ← N-O-I-T-A-T-I-P-I-C-E-R-P    1

**SILLY ACT:** Pretend to be caught in a sudden rain shower.

**DISPROPORTIONATE** ← E-T-A-N-O-I-T-R-O-P-O-R-P-S-I-D    6

**SILLY ACT:** Mime something big with one hand and something small with the other.

# Hard
## LEVEL

## Points

**ENTREPRENEURIAL** ← L-A-I-R-U-E-N-E-R-P-E-R-T-N-E    1

**SILLY ACT:** Pitch your new business idea to an audience.

**ENVIRONMENTALIST** ← T-S-I-L-A-T-N-E-M-N-O-R-I-V-N-E    1

**SILLY ACT:** Mime planting a tree and patting down the soil.

**EXCEPTIONALITY** ← Y-T-I-L-A-N-O-I-T-P-E-C-X-E    1

**SILLY ACT:** Pretend to be a juggler showing off exceptional skills.

**EXTRACURRICULAR** ← R-A-L-U-C-I-R-R-U-C-A-R-T-X-E    1

**SILLY ACT:** Mime playing a sport or an instrument.

**DISTINGUISHABLE** ← E-L-B-A-H-S-I-U-G-N-I-T-S-I-D    6

**SILLY ACT:** Act like a detective, scrutinizing something with an imaginary magnifying glass.

# Hard

## LEVEL

**Points**

**IMPENETRABLE** ← E-L-B-A-R-T-E-N-E-P-M-I    1

**SILLY ACT:** Pretend to be a superhero with an impenetrable shield.

**MISUNDERSTANDING** ← G-N-I-D-N-A-T-S-R-E-D-N-U-S-I-M    1

**SILLY ACT:** Mime a classic game of telephone gone wrong.

**NONNEGOTIABLE** ← E-L-B-A-I-T-O-G-E-N-N-O-N    1

**SILLY ACT:** Cross your arms and shake your head stubbornly.

**PHOTOGRAPHICAL** ← L-A-C-I-H-P-A-R-G-O-T-O-H-P    1

**SILLY ACT:** Pretend to be a photographer, taking pictures from all angles.

**OVERCOMPENSATE** ← E-T-A-S-N-E-P-M-O-C-R-E-V-O    6

**SILLY ACT:** Act like you're lifting a heavy object that suddenly becomes as light as a feather.

# Hard

### LEVEL

## Points

**PSYCHOLOGICAL** ⬅ L-A-C-I-G-O-L-O-H-C-Y-S-P    1

**SILLY ACT:** Sit down and act like you're psychoanalyzing someone.

**REMINISCENCES** ⬅ S-E-C-N-E-C-S-I-N-I-M-E-R    1

**SILLY ACT:** Act like you're an old person, recalling memories.

**REPRESENTATIVE** ⬅ E-V-I-T-A-T-N-E-S-E-R-P-E-R    1

**SILLY ACT:** Pretend to give a speech as a representative.

**SPECTACULARLY** ⬅ Y-L-R-A-L-U-C-A-T-C-E-P-S    1

**SILLY ACT:** Act like you're watching a spectacular fireworks show.

**RECONSIDERATION** ⬅ N-O-I-T-A-R-E-D-I-S-N-O-C-E-R    6

**SILLY ACT:** Pretend to ponder deeply, then suddenly change your mind.

# Hard
### LEVEL

## Points

**UNSYMMETRICAL** ✎ L-A-C-I-R-T-E-M-M-Y-S-N-U  1

**SILLY ACT:** Try to balance in a funny asymmetrical pose.

**VOLUNTEERISM** ✎ M-S-I-R-E-E-T-N-U-L-O-V  1

**SILLY ACT:** Mime doing different kinds of community service.

**UNFATHOMABLE** ✎ E-L-B-A-M-O-H-T-A-F-N-U  1

**SILLY ACT:** Pretend to be diving deeper and deeper into the ocean.

**UNDERESTIMATION** ✎ N-O-I-T-A-M-I-T-S-E-R-E-D-N-U  1

**SILLY ACT:** Pretend to pick up something you think is light but is actually heavy.

**INCONSEQUENTIAL** ✎ L-A-I-T-N-E-U-Q-E-S-N-O-C-N-I  6

**SILLY ACT:** Shrug and make a dismissive facial expression, as if something doesn't matter at all.

# Hard

### LEVEL

## Points

**INTERPRETATIVE** ✏ E-V-I-T-A-T-E-R-P-R-E-T-N-I    1

**SILLY ACT:** Interpretively dance to an imaginary song.

**DISAPPOINTMENT** ✏ T-N-E-M-T-N-I-O-P-P-A-S-I-D    1

**SILLY ACT:** React to opening an imaginary disappointing gift.

**ENTERTAINMENT** ✏ T-N-E-M-N-I-A-T-R-E-T-N-E    1

**SILLY ACT:** Pretend to be a stand-up comedian telling jokes.

**ELECTROLYTES** ✏ S-E-T-Y-L-O-R-T-C-E-L-E    1

**SILLY ACT:** Pretend to be chugging a sports drink and feeling energized.

**COMMUNICATION** ✏ N-O-I-T-A-C-I-N-U-M-M-O-C    6

**SILLY ACT:** Act like you're in a silent film, expressing something without words.

# Hard
## LEVEL

## Points

**UNBELIEVABLE** ← E-L-B-A-V-E-I-L-E-B-N-U     1

**SILLY ACT:** Act out being amazed by a magic trick.

**MANUFACTURER** ← R-E-R-U-T-C-A-F-U-N-A-M     1

**SILLY ACT:** Mime assembling a complicated machine.

**THERMOMETER** ← R-E-T-E-M-O-M-R-E-H-T     1

**SILLY ACT:** Pretend to take the temperature of a giant beast.

**RECONCILIATION** ← N-O-I-T-A-I-L-I-C-N-O-C-E-R     1

**SILLY ACT:** Act out a dramatic makeup between two friends.

**INCONVENIENCE** ← E-C-N-E-I-N-E-V-N-O-C-N-I     6

**SILLY ACT:** Act like you're in a hurry but keep getting interrupted by minor annoyances.

# Hard
## LEVEL

**Points**

**CONSEQUENCE** ✎ E-C-N-E-U-Q-E-S-N-O-C     1

**SILLY ACT:** Act out a silly chain reaction of events.

**PRESCRIPTION** ✎ N-O-I-T-P-I-R-C-S-E-R-P     1

**SILLY ACT:** Pretend to read an eye chart as an optometrist.

**RESPONSIBLE** ✎ E-L-B-I-S-N-O-P-S-E-R     1

**SILLY ACT:** Mime cleaning up an imaginary room very responsibly.

**ANTHROPOLOGY** ✎ Y-G-O-L-O-P-O-R-H-T-N-A     1

**SILLY ACT:** Pretend you have discovered a new civilization.

**OUTRAGEOUSLY** ✎ Y-L-S-U-O-E-G-A-R-T-U-O     **6**

**SILLY ACT:** Pretend to be a mime stuck in an outrageous situation.

# Hard

**LEVEL**

## Points

**ELECTRICITY** ⬅ Y-T-I-C-I-R-T-C-E-L-E     1

**SILLY ACT:** Do a quick "electric slide" dance.

**MANUFACTURE** ⬅ E-R-U-T-C-A-F-U-N-A-M     1

**SILLY ACT:** Pretend to operate an imaginary assembly line.

**EXPRESSIONIST** ⬅ T-S-I-N-O-I-S-S-E-R-P-X-E     1

**SILLY ACT:** Make three dramatically different facial expressions.

**SURROUNDINGS** ⬅ S-G-N-I-D-N-U-O-R-R-U-S     1

**SILLY ACT:** Mime exploring a new environment with awe.

**CONSTELLATION** ⬅ N-O-I-T-A-L-L-E-T-S-N-O-C     6

**SILLY ACT:** Mime connecting stars to form a constellation in the sky.

# Hard

LEVEL

## Points

**AUTOMATICALLY** ⟵ Y-L-L-A-C-I-T-A-M-O-T-U-A  1

**SILLY ACT:** Act like a robot performing various tasks.

**RESTAURATEUR** ⟵ R-U-E-T-A-R-U-A-T-S-E-R  1

**SILLY ACT:** Mimic taking multiple food orders at once, getting busier and busier!

**EXTRAVAGANZA** ⟵ A-Z-N-A-G-A-V-A-R-T-X-E  1

**SILLY ACT:** Do a quick, over-the-top celebration dance.

**TRANSPORTING** ⟵ G-N-I-T-R-O-P-S-N-A-R-T  1

**SILLY ACT:** Mime pushing a heavy object to move it out of the way.

**ACCOMMODATING** ⟵ G-N-I-T-A-D-O-M-M-O-C-C-A  6

**SILLY ACT:** Pretend to make room for imaginary people in a crowded space.

# Hard
## LEVEL

## Points

**CONCENTRATION** ← N-O-I-T-A-R-T-N-E-C-N-O-C    1

**SILLY ACT:** Pretend you are a meditating monk.

**OVERWROUGHT** ← T-H-G-U-O-R-W-R-E-V-O    1

**SILLY ACT:** Pretend to be pulling at your hair in frustration.

**INTERPRETATION** ← N-O-I-T-A-T-E-R-P-R-E-T-N-I    1

**SILLY ACT:** Pretend to be a mime interpreting a scene.

**DISAPPOINTMENT** ← T-N-E-M-T-N-I-O-P-P-A-S-I-D    1

**SILLY ACT:** Show an exaggerated frown and then shake it off with a smile.

**UNCONTROLLABLE** ← E-L-B-A-L-L-O-R-T-N-O-C-N-U    6

**SILLY ACT:** Pretend you're trying to control a wacky, wobbling, inflatable tube man.

# Hard
## LEVEL

**Points**

**UNCONVENTIONAL** ← L-A-N-O-I-T-N-E-V-N-O-C-N-U    1

**SILLY ACT:** Do a silly, unconventional dance.

**DIFFERENTIATION** ← N-O-I-T-A-I-T-N-E-R-E-F-F-I-D    1

**SILLY ACT:** Mime out dramatically different expressions or poses.

**TECHNOLOGICAL** ← L-A-C-I-G-O-L-O-N-H-C-E-T    1

**SILLY ACT:** Pretend to be a robot doing the robot dance.

**INAPPROPRIATE** ← E-T-A-I-R-P-O-R-P-P-A-N-I    1

**SILLY ACT:** Act as if you've done something wrong, and then correct it.

**COLLABORATIVE** ← E-V-I-T-A-R-O-B-A-L-L-O-C    6

**SILLY ACT:** Pretend to be working on a team project, passing imaginary items.

# Hard
**LEVEL**

## Points

**SIMPLIFICATION** ⬅ N-O-I-T-A-C-I-F-I-L-P-M-I-S    1

**SILLY ACT:** Pretend to simplify a complex imaginary machine into a single button.

**DISTINGUISHED** ⬅ D-E-H-S-I-U-G-N-I-T-S-I-D    1

**SILLY ACT:** Pretend to adjust a bow tie and tip an imaginary top hat.

**CONGRATULATIONS** ⬅ S-N-O-I-T-A-L-U-T-A-R-G-N-O-C    1

**SILLY ACT:** Pretend to throw confetti in the air.

**UNIVERSITIES** ⬅ S-E-I-T-I-S-R-E-V-I-N-U    1

**SILLY ACT:** Mime throwing a graduation cap in the air.

**TRANSPORTATION** ⬅ N-O-I-T-A-T-R-O-P-S-N-A-R-T    **6**

**SILLY ACT:** Mime various forms of transportation, from a car to a plane.

# Hard
## LEVEL

**Points**

### UNUSUAL ⬅ L-A-U-S-U-N-U                     1
**SILLY ACT:** Pretend you're an alien from another planet!

### OVERCOME ⬅ E-M-O-C-R-E-V-O                  1
**SILLY ACT:** Act like you're climbing a steep mountain!

### DEMONSTRATION ⬅ N-O-I-T-A-R-T-S-N-O-M-E-D   1
**SILLY ACT:** Mime demonstrating how to use an imaginary object.

### UNDERSTANDING ⬅ G-N-I-D-N-A-T-S-R-E-D-N-U   1
**SILLY ACT:** Tap your forehead, then open your hands out as if sharing knowledge.

### COLLABORATION ⬅ N-O-I-T-A-R-O-B-A-L-L-O-C   6
**SILLY ACT:** Pretend to be working on a team project with lots of high-fives.

# Hard
## LEVEL

**Points**

## APPRECIATE ⇐ E-T-A-I-C-E-R-P-P-A
**SILLY ACT:** Act like you're receiving an award!

1

## EXCEPTION ⇐ N-O-I-T-P-E-C-X-E
**SILLY ACT:** Pretend you're an exception to gravity and start floating!

1

## INFLUENCE ⇐ E-C-N-E-U-L-F-N-I
**SILLY ACT:** Pretend you're a magician influencing people with your tricks!

1

## TERRITORY ⇐ Y-R-O-T-I-R-R-E-T
**SILLY ACT:** Pretend you're marking your territory like a wild animal!

1

## ABUNDANCE ⇐ E-C-N-A-D-N-U-B-A
**SILLY ACT:** Act like you're picking up coins from a treasure chest!

6

# Hard

## LEVEL

**Points**

## SPECTACULAR ⟵ R-A-L-U-C-A-T-C-E-P-S    1

**SILLY ACT:** Pretend you're a spectacular fireworks display!

## DISTINGUISH ⟵ H-S-I-U-G-N-I-T-S-I-D    1

**SILLY ACT:** Act like a detective distinguishing clues!

## SUBSTANTIAL ⟵ L-A-I-T-N-A-T-S-B-U-S    1

**SILLY ACT:** Pretend to lift a substantial weight!

## INTERPRET ⟵ T-E-R-P-R-E-T-N-I    1

**SILLY ACT:** Act like you're interpreting complicated sign language!

## ACCIDENTALLY ⟵ Y-L-L-A-T-N-E-D-I-C-C-A    6

**SILLY ACT:** Pretend you've accidentally walked into a spider web!

# Hard

## LEVEL

## Points

### UNPREDICTABLE ⇦ E-L-B-A-T-C-I-D-E-R-P-N-U    1
**SILLY ACT:** Pretend to be a fortune teller!

### ENCOURAGEMENT ⇦ T-N-E-M-E-G-A-R-U-O-C-N-E    1
**SILLY ACT:** Act like you're encouraging a friend to leap!

### PARTICIPATION ⇦ N-O-I-T-A-P-I-C-I-T-R-A-P    1
**SILLY ACT:** Act like you're participating in a round of applause at a concert!

### OVERWHELMING ⇦ G-N-I-M-L-E-H-W-R-E-V-O    1
**SILLY ACT:** Pretend you're being overwhelmed by a tickle attack!

### CONVERSATION ⇦ N-O-I-T-A-S-R-E-V-N-O-C    6
**SILLY ACT:** Pretend to have a conversation with an invisible friend!

# Hard
## LEVEL

**Points**

**ACCOMMODATION** ⟵ N-O-I-T-A-D-O-M-M-O-C-C-A    1

    **SILLY ACT:** Pretend to arrange a miniature hotel room!

**CONSIDERATION** ⟵ N-O-I-T-A-R-E-D-I-S-N-O-C    1

    **SILLY ACT:** Act like you're considering between two delicious foods!

**APPREHENSIVE** ⟵ E-V-I-S-N-E-H-E-R-P-P-A    1

    **SILLY ACT:** Pretend you're nervously waiting for your turn on a roller coaster!

**UNDERESTIMATE** ⟵ E-T-A-M-I-T-S-E-R-E-D-N-U    1

    **SILLY ACT:** Pretend to lift something heavy only to find it's light as a feather!

**RESPONSIBILITY** ⟵ Y-T-I-L-I-B-I-S-N-O-P-S-E-R    **6**

    **SILLY ACT:** Pretend you're a superhero, flying from place to place to save people in need!

## Share Your Thoughts:

We hope you're having a blast with **The Reverse Spelling Challenge!** If you're enjoying the game, please leave us a review so others can discover this book and join the fun. Your feedback is invaluable!

If you have suggestions on how we can improve, please email us at **hello@tworavensbooks.com.**

## Show Off Your Skills:

Parents and Guardians, we'd love to see you and your young reverse-spellers in action!

Consider sharing a video on social media using the hashtag **#TheReverseSpellingChallenge.**

Let's spread the fun and encourage more families to take the challenge!

Find more humorously educational books like this at **TwoRavensBooks.com**

**TWORAVENS**

B O O K S

# Collectible imprints
# for little learners & readers

## Xander & Rem

Children's Coloring & Activity Books

## Xander's Perch

CHILDREN'S FICTION BOOKS

## Two Little Ravens

CHILDREN'S NON-FICTION BOOKS

www.ingramcontent.com/pod-product-compliance
Lightning Source LLC
Chambersburg PA
CBHW051552120626
46551CB00013B/1485